YOU
TELL
ME

JANETTA OTTER-BARRY BOOKS

Roger McGough poems copyright © Roger McGough1969, 1971, 1973,
1974, 1976, 1979, 1981, 2001 and 2015
*PC Plod and the Catnapper, The Totally Inoffensive Children's Poem,
Lost and Found, PC Plod Stumbles Over the Words, Big Arth,
Uncle Sean, You Tell Me* copyright © 2015
Michael Rosen poems copyright © Michael Rosen1979, 2001 and 2015
The Talent Show, Wrong, Where Broccoli Comes From copyright © 2015
Illustrations copyright © Korky Paul 2015

Original edition first published in Great Britain in hardback in 1979
by Kestrel Books and in paperback in 1981 by Puffin Books

This revised paperback edition first published in Great Britain and in the
USA in 2015 by Frances Lincoln Children's Books,
74-77 White Lion Street, London N1 9PF
www.franceslincoln.com

A catalogue record for this book is available from the British Library.

ISBN 978-1-84780-444-0

Printed in Croydon, Surrey, UK by CPI Bookmarque Ltd.

1 3 5 7 9 8 6 4 2

YOU TELL ME

Poems by
ROGER McGOUGH
MICHAEL ROSEN

Drawings by
KORKY PAUL

F

FRANCES LINCOLN
CHILDREN'S BOOKS

Contents

You Tell Me

Here are the football results:
League Division Fun
Manchester United won, Manchester City lost.
Crystal Palace 2, Buckingham Palace 1
Wolves 8 A cheese roll and had a cup of tea 2
Chelsea 6 Up-in-a-bowl 2
Crawley Town 1 Creepy Town 1
Bury 1 Now-I-can't-find-it 2
Brighton 1 Cloudy 2
Torquay 1 Worquay 1
Burnley 1 So-Lee-says-Ouch 2
Norwich 1 Porridge 1
Wimbledon 4 Tennis 2
West Ham versus Sliced Ham – match postponed
Newcastle's Heaven Sunderland's a very nice place 2
Ipswhich one? You tell me.

A Good Poem

I like a good poem
one with lots of fighting
in it. Blood, and the
clanging of armour. Poems

against Scotland are good,
and poems that defeat
the French with crossbows.
I don't like poems that

aren't about anything.
Sonnets are wet and
a waste of time.
Also poems that don't

know how to rhyme.
If I was a poem
I'd play football and
get picked for England.

What's Your Name?

When they said
'What's your name?'
I used to say,
'Michael Rosen
Rosen
R, O, S, E, N
with a silent "Q" as in rhubarb.'

And they'd say,
'That's not very funny.'

PC Plod and the Catnapper

For several months, Liverpool was held in the grip of fear
by a catnapper most devilish. A foul beast
who roamed the streets after dark looking for strays.
Finding one, he would tickle it behind the ears
before luring it into the back of his white van
with the promise of mouse-flavoured biscuits.
Hardly a night passed without somebody's
pet tabby being driven off to who knows where.

The public were warned
That after lights out
To keep their cats in
(But cats love their nights out).

Nine o'clock on the evening of January 11th
sees PC Plod on the corner of Brownlow Hill
and Mount Street disguised as a ginger tom.
It is part of a daring plan to catch the catnapper.
For though it is a wet and moonless night
Plod is cheered in the knowledge
that the whole of the Merseyside Police Force
is on the beat that night disguised as pussy cats.
Not ten minutes earlier, a blue tortoiseshell, (WPC Hodges)
had scampered past on her way to Clayton Square.

For Plod, the night passed uneventfully,
and so in the morning he was horrified to learn
that no less than fourteen policemen and policewomen
had been tickled and kidnapped during the night.

The public were terrified
The Commissioner aghast
Something had to be done
And fast.

11

PC Plod (wise as a brace of owls)
submitted an idea so audacious,
so startling in its vision,
that the Chief Constable gasped
before ordering all cats in the city
to be disguised as cops. The plan worked
and the White Van Catnapper was heard of no more.

> *Cats and coppers*
> *Like peas in a pod*
> *To a grateful public*
> *Plod was God.*

So next time you are up in Liverpool
Take a closer look at that policeman on point duty.
He might well be a Siamese bobtail.

Rodge Said

Rodge said,
'Teachers – they want it all ways –
You're jumping up and down on a chair
or something
and they grab hold of you and say,
"Would you do that sort of thing in your own home?"

'So you say, "No."
And they say,
"Well don't do it here then."

'But if you say, "Yes, I do it at home."
they say,
"Well, we don't want that sort of thing going on here
thank you very much."

'Teachers – they get you all ways,'
Rodge said.

When We Go Over

When we go over
to my grandad's
he falls asleep.

While he's asleep
he snores.

When he wakes up,
he says,
'Did I snore?
did I snore?
did I snore?'

Everybody says, 'No,
you didn't snore.'

Why do we lie to him?

The Lesson

(P.G. Contains scenes of cartoon violence which some adults may find unsettling.)

Chaos ruled OK in the classroom
as bravely the teacher walked in
the nooligans ignored him
his voice was lost in the din

'The theme for today is violence
and homework will be set
I'm going to teach you a lesson
one that you'll never forget'

He picked on a boy who was shouting
and throttled him then and there
then garrotted the girl behind him
(the one with the grotty hair)

Then sword in hand he hacked his way
between the chattering rows
'First come, first severed' he declared
'fingers, feet or toes'

He threw the sword at a latecomer
it struck with deadly aim
then pulling out a shotgun
he continued with his game

The first blast cleared the back row
(where those who skive hang out)
they collapsed like rubber dinghies
when the plug's pulled out

'Please may I leave the room sir?'
a trembling vandal enquired
'Of course you may' said teacher
put the gun to his temple and fired

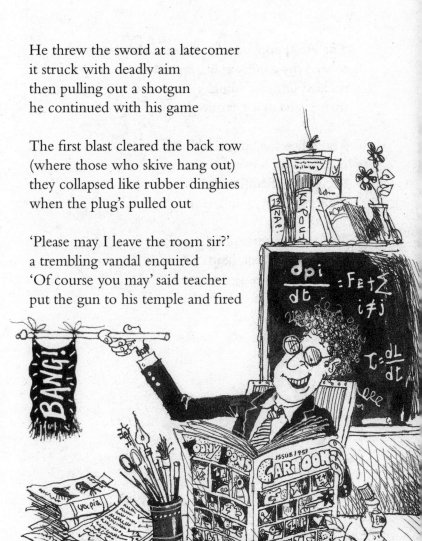

The Head popped a head round the doorway
to see why a din was being made
nodded understandingly
then tossed in a grenade

And when the ammo was well spent
with blood on every chair
Silence shuffled forward
with its hands up in the air

The teacher surveyed the carnage
the dying and the dead
He waggled a finger severely
'Now let that be a lesson' he said.

The Totally Inoffensive Children's Poem

There are no guns in this poem
Even cartoon ones that go pop!

No religion, no fear.
No priests or mullahs lurking in here

No smut or innuendo
I soon showed sex the door

No mention of alcohol or drugs
It keeps well within the law

References to weight?
Of course this poem has no weight.
It is totally inoffensive.

Chivvy

Grown-ups say things like:
Speak up
Don't talk with your mouth full
Don't stare
Don't point
Don't pick your nose
Sit up
Say please
Less noise
Shut the door behind you
Don't drag your feet
Haven't you got a hankie?

Take your hands out of your pockets
Pull your socks up
Stand up straight
Say thank you
Don't interrupt
No one thinks you're funny
Take your elbows off the table ...

Can't you make your own
mind up about anything?

Some People

Some people
are always passing comments.
They say to me:
hallo hairy
your hands are huge
do you know your eyes pop out?
you're a monster
you aren't half white
your fingers are like sausages
you walk like a bear
is that thing on your chin a wart?

Nooligan

I'm a nooligan
dont give a toss
in our class
I'm the boss
(well, one of them)

I'm a nooligan
got a nard 'ead
step out of line
and you're dead
(well, bleedin)

I'm a nooligan
I spray me name
all over town
footballs me game
(well, watchin)

I'm a nooligan
violence is fun
gonna be a nassassin
or a nired gun
(well, a nactor)

Streemin

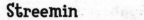

Im in the botom streme
Which meens Im not brigth
dont like readin
cant hardly write

but all these divishns
arnt reely fair
look at the cemtery
no streemin there

Mart Was my Best Friend

Mart was my best friend.
I thought he was great,
but one day he tried to do for me.

I had a hat – a woolly one
and I loved that hat.
It was warm and tight.
My mum had knitted it
and I wore it everywhere.

One day me and Mart were out
and we were standing at a bus-stop
and suddenly
he goes and grabs my hat
and chucked it over the wall.
He thought I was going to go in there
and get it out.
He thought he'd make me do that
because he knew I liked that hat so much
I wouldn't be able to stand being without it.

He was right –
I could hardly bear it.
I was really scared I'd never get it back.
But I never let on.
I never showed it on my face.
I just waited.

'Aren't you going to get your hat?'
he says.
'Your hat's gone,' he says.
'Your hat's over the wall.'
I looked the other way.

But I could still feel on my head
how he had pulled it off.
'Your hat's over the wall,' he says.
I didn't say a thing.

Then the bus came round the corner
at the end of the road.

If I go home without my hat
I'm going to walk through the door
and Mum's going to say,
'Where's your hat?'
and if I say,
'It's over the wall,'
she's going to say,
'What's it doing there?'
And I'm going to say,
'Mart chucked it over,'
and she's going to say,
'Why didn't you go for it?'
and what am I going to say then?
What am I going to say then?

The bus was coming up.
'Aren't you going over for your hat?
There won't be another bus for ages,'
Mart says.

The bus was coming closer.
'You've lost your hat now,'
Mart says.

The bus stopped.
I got on
Mart got on.
The bus moved off.

'You've lost your hat,' Mart says.

'You've lost your hat,' Mart says.

Two stops ahead, was ours.
'Are you going indoors without it?' Mart says.
I didn't say a thing.

The bus stopped.

Mart got up
and dashed downstairs.
He'd got off one stop early.
I got off when we got to our stop.

I went home
walked through the door.
'Where's your hat?' Mum says.
'Over a wall,' I said.
'What's it doing there?' she says.
'Mart chucked it over there,' I said.
'But you haven't left it there, have you?' she says.
'Yes,' I said.
'Well don't you ever come asking me to make you
anything like that again.
You make me tired, you do.'

Later,
I was drinking some orange juice.
The front door-bell rang.
It was Mart.
He had the hat in his hand.
He handed it to me – and went.

I shut the front door –
put on the hat
and walked into the kitchen.

Mum looked up.
'You don't need to wear your hat indoors do you?'
she said.
'I will for a bit,' I said.
And I did.

Mart's Advice

Mart's advice:
If someone's acting big with you,
if someone's bossing you about
look very hard at one of their ears.
Keep your eyes fixed on it.
Don't let up.
Stare at it as if it was
a mouldy apple.
Keep staring.
Don't blink.

After a bit
you'll see their hand
go creeping up to touch it.
They're saying to themselves
'What's wrong with my ear?'

At that moment
you know you've won.

Smile.

A Bad Habit

'Cigarette, Mike?' they say,
'I don't smoke,' I say.
'Haven't you got any bad habits?' they say.
'Yes,' I say, 'I chew bus tickets.'

I can't stop it.
The conductor gives me a ticket
and before I know I've done it
I've rolled it up
and I'm sucking on it like a cigarette.

I hold it with my fingers.
I roll it.
I flick it.
I hold it in my lips.

But there's a snag with my bus-ticket cigarettes:
they go soggy,
they go gooey
and I nibble
and I bite
and I chew –
my bus tickets get shorter and shorter
and before I know it I've done it
all I've got is a ball of soggy paper
rolling round my mouth.

Disgusting.

Smokers buy pills to stop their filthy habit.
All I've got is bus inspectors.

You see, once, not long ago,
I was on a bus
and my ticket was in a ball
rolling round my mouth
and suddenly – above me –
there's the inspector.
'Tickets, please,' he says,
and there's me – nibble, nibble, nibble
on the mushed up ball of paper in my mouth.

He wants to see my ticket.
Of course he can see my ticket
if he doesn't mind inspecting
a little ball of mush.

So I say, 'Yes, you can see my ticket,'
and I stuck my finger in my mouth
and hauled out the blob.

He looks at it.
He looks at me.
It's sitting there on the end of my finger.
'What's that?' he says,
'My ticket,' I said,
'What did you have for breakfast?' he says,
'Corn Flakes,' I said.
'Mmm,' he says,
'Did you ever think of having a slice or two of toast,
as well, old son,' he says,
'and maybe you won't be so tempted by our tickets.'
And he left it at that.

But it's very hard to break the habit,
even after a warning like that.
Got any ideas?

Snipers

When I was knee-high to a table-top,
Uncle Ted came home from Burma.
He was the youngest of seven brothers
so the street borrowed extra bunting
and whitewashed him a welcome.

All the relations made the pilgrimage,
including us, laughed, sang, made a fuss.
He was as brown as a chairleg,
drank tea out of a white mug the size of my head,
and said next to nowt.

But every few minutes he would scan
the ceiling nervously, hands begin to shake.
'For snipers,' everyone later agreed.
'A difficult habit to break.'

Sometimes when the two of us were alone,
he'd have a snooze after dinner
and I'd keep an eye open for Japs.
Of course, he didn't know this
and the tanner he'd give me before I went
was for keeping quiet,
but I liked to think it was money well spent.

Being Uncle Ted's secret bodyguard
had its advantages, the pay was good
and the hours were short, but even so,
the novelty soon wore off, and instead,
I started school and became an infant.

Later, I learned that he was in a mental home.
'Needn't tell anybody . . . Nothing serious
. . . Delayed shock . . . Usual sort of thing
. . . Completely cured now the doctors say.'
The snipers came down from the ceiling
but they didn't go away.

Over the next five years they picked off
three of his brothers; one of whom was my father.
No glory, no citations,
Bang! straight through the heart.

Uncle Ted's married now, with a family.
He doesn't say much, but each night after tea,
he still dozes fitfully in his favourite armchair.
He keeps out of the sun, and listens now and then
for the tramp tramp tramp of the Colonel Bogeymen.
He knows damn well he's still at war,
just that the snipers aren't Japs any more.

Busy Day

Pop in
pop out
pop over the road
pop out for a walk
pop in for a talk
pop down to the shop
can't stop
got to pop

got to pop?

pop where?
pop what?

well
I've got to
pop round
pop up
pop in to town
pop out and see
pop in for tea
pop down to the shop
can't stop
got to pop

got to pop?

pop where?
pop what?

well
I've got to
pop in
pop out
pop over the road
pop out for a walk
pop in for a talk…

The Hardest Thing to Do in the World

The Hardest Thing to Do in the World
is stand in the hot sun
at the end of a long queue for ice creams
watching all the people who've just bought theirs
coming away from the queue
giving their ice creams their very first lick.

The Talent Show

It was going to be the talent show
at Barking Primary School.
Each of us had an act to do;
mine was: play the fool.

I would look all tired and giddy
like I was going to faint.
I'd fall over in one big heap,
face down in some paint.

My friend Jimmy, 'The Doughnut Jam'
was going to juggle cakes;
My friend Mary, 'The Biscuit Crumb'
was going to juggle snakes.

So I'm watching everyone else
with Fizzy at my side –
Fizzy is my little dog
and now he was trying to hide.

Then Mrs Bones, my teacher, waved;
I was ready for the off,
when underneath my chair, I heard
little Fizzy give a cough.

In a rush he flew straight at the stage,
I wondered what was wrong.
Then he grabbed the microphone in his paw
and started to sing a song.

He sang about a ship's captain
whose name was Benny Brown
and when he went to meet the queen
his trousers they fell down.

Then Fizzy stopped and took a bow –
I promise I tell no lies.
You know very well what happened next
Fizzy won first prize.

That's what happened at Barking.
Now you really know.
Each of us had an act to do
but Fizzy stole the show.

Down Behind the Dustbin

Down behind the dustbin
I met a dog called Ted.
'Leave me alone,' he says,
'I'm just going to bed.'

Down behind the dustbin
I met a dog called Felicity.
'It's a bit dark here,' she said,
'They've cut off the electricity.'

Down behind the dustbin
I met a dog called Roger.
'Do you own this bin?' I said.
'No. I'm only the lodger.'

Ian said,
Down behind the dustbin
I met a dog called Sue.
'What are you doing here?' I said.
'I've got nothing else to do.'

Down behind the dustbin
I met a dog called Anne.
'I'm just off now,' she said,
'to see a dog about a man.'

Down behind the dustbin
I met a dog called Jack.
'Are you going anywhere?' I said.
'No. I'm just coming back.'

Down behind the dustbin
I met a dog called Billy.
'I'm not talking to you,' I said,
'if you're going to be silly.'

Down behind the dustbin
I met a dog called Barry.
He tried to take the bin away
but it was too heavy to carry.

Down behind the dustbin
I met a dog called Mary.
'I wish I wasn't a dog,' she said,
'I wish I was a canary.'

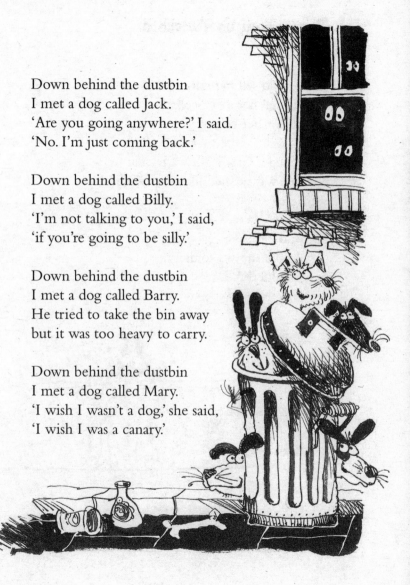

Three Tongue Twisters

If he could sell her salt,
I could sell her a salt-cellar
for salt for her celery

I watched a Car-Wash wash a car
I wish I was washed like Car-Washes
wash cars

She said
should she show a soldier
her shoulder?

One Day When I was Young

One day when I was young
there was going to be a fancy dress show.
For a while I couldn't think
who to go as.
I didn't have any cowboy hats
or moustaches or angel's wings.
I couldn't think what to go as.

Then I suddenly thought,
'I could go as My Mum.'
I could get up in an old skirt of hers,
hat and coat –
and there I'd be – My Mum.

Mum thought it was a really good idea
and she gave me her old green skirt
she didn't wear any more
and a horrible fawn coat-jacket thing
with big shoulders and gold buttons.
I wore shorts underneath the skirt
no socks, just sandals
and I put on a straw hat
and Mum found me an old black shiny handbag.
Dressed up like that I now had to get to the hall
where the show was on.

I waited till it was dark
and then ran through the streets
holding the skirt up around my knees.

When I got there, it had already begun.
And I couldn't quite understand
what was going on,
because, you see, all the rest of the children
were standing around in the hall very very still,
and the woman in charge was going round
putting her face very close to the children's faces
and trying to make them laugh.

So there was Richard Russell
who had a beard, a black shirt
a pair of his sister's tights on
and one of those white frilly things
you put round birthday cakes –
he had round his neck
and the woman was right up against his nose
and saying in a very high voice:
'Hallo Willy. Willy Willy Shakespeare.
Have you written a play today, Willy?'

Someone said I had to go and stand out there
and I wasn't to laugh
and I'd win.
So I went out there
and she went on round the hall
talking in this very high voice:
'Hallo Big Ears.
Where's Noddy?
Beep, beep in his little car is he?'
And they were creasing up in giggles
all over the place.

Then she got to me.
And she said,
'Who are you?' she said,
'My Mum,' I said.
And everyone in the hall laughed.
They laughed and laughed.
At first I thought they were laughing
because I had make a good joke
and then I saw that they were laughing
because they thought I was stupid.
That annoyed me.

So this woman who had also laughed at me,
now tried to make me laugh
by putting her big puffy red face close to mine and saying,
'Are you My Mum? Oh you are looking nice today,
          Mummy.'
Well obviously I didn't think it was very funny –
in fact I thought it was pathetic.
But she kept at it.
'Hallo Mummy. Mummy can I have some sweets
please?'

So I didn't laugh.
But the others did.
But I didn't win though.
I think Big Ears won.
He got a box of chocolates and a pack of cards.
Then we all went home.

As we were walking down the road
away from the place,
a boy called Terence,
who wasn't allowed to play with me
because his mum said I was common,
he said, 'You're daft, you are.
Why did you come dressed up as your mother?
You wouldn't find your mother in Madame Tussaud's
          Waxworks,
would you?'

When I got in,
I asked Mum what a Waxworks was.
She told me it was a place
where they make big life-size wax dolls
of famous people.
Then I said, 'I didn't win, Mum,
because you're not famous enough to be a waxwork.'
'Oh well, never mind,' she says,
'we can't all be famous can we?' she says.
But I said, 'But no – don't you see –
I didn't laugh. I should've won. I didn't laugh.'

Gruesome

I was sitting in the sitting room
toying with some toys
when from a door marked: 'GRUESOME'
There came a GRUESOME noise.

Cautiously I opened it
and there to my surprise
a little GRUE lay sitting
with tears in its eyes.

'Oh little GRUE please tell me
what is it ails thee so?'
'Well I'm so small,' he sobbed,
'GRUESSES don't want to know.'

'Exercises are the answer,
Each morning you must DO SOME.'
He thanked me, smiled,
and do you know what?
The very next day he…

A Long Time Ago

A long time ago
there was a man who lived round our way
and he said:
'When I die,
I don't want to be buried in the ground
I want to be buried in the air.'
So he set about making sure
he would be buried in the air.
He got people to build him a big yellow tower.
He said, 'I want to be buried halfway up this tower.'
Not long after, he died.
When they came to bury him
they decided that they didn't want to bury him
in the air, halfway up the tower,
so they buried him in the ground instead
and there was nothing on earth he could do about it.
But the tower's still there
and everyone knows it was built for the man
who wanted to be buried in the air
but couldn't make sure he would be.

Lost and Found

'Welcome to the Lost and Found
Step inside and look around

Enjoy the visit but take extra care
There's a boa constrictor loose somewhere

On buses and trains you wouldn't believe
The crazy things that passengers leave

A dodgem car, I kid you not
Hot water-bottle full, but no longer hot

Leopard-skin tights for the fuller figure
A pineapple carved with the face of Mick Jagger

Deflating slowly, a lead balloon
A barrel of monkeys and a red baboon

Bikes and skateboards by the score
Two bags of steaming horse manure

Rucksacks, tents and rolled-up beds
If they weren't screwed on they'd lose their heads

Stop for a moment, do I hear a strange hissing?
Let me just check there's nobody missing

No, all present and correct I'm glad to say
The snake has probably slithered away

Where was I? Oh yes, an electric chair
Dozens of dolls and a huge teddy bear

A dodgy piano and a didgeridoo
A doddery dog and a portable loo

A ventriloquist's dummy at a loss for words
Three French hens and four calling birds

What's that noise? A strangling sound?
It's the giant snake. Don't turn around

Run for your lives, and I'm sorry to say
We're definitely closed for the rest of the day.'

Fork Week

You're going to lay the table.
You go to the drawer to get the knives, forks and
spoons.
You find the forks
you find the spoons
but the knives – they've all gone.
You look everywhere
the sink, the table, the draining board
but they've all gone.

A few days later – it's the same
only it's the spoons this time
and all the knives have come back.

My brother,
he's worked it out,
he says they take it in turns to disappear.
'It's all right,' he says,
'We won't see another fork till Thursday,
it's Fork Week.'

Bucket

every evening after tea
grandad would take his bucket for a walk

an empty bucket

when I asked him why
he said it was because it was easier to carry
than a full one

grandad had
an answer
for everything

Railings

towards the end of his tether
grandad
at the drop of a hat
would paint the railings

overnight
we became famous
all over the neighbourhood
for our smart railings

(and our dirty hats)

Scratch

I know a cat that scratched a baby.
It's prowling around the legs
of the baby's mother
looking for a stroke.

It's an animal.
Animals don't know
we don't stroke
people who hurt.

Scram!

It gets out
through the same window
it got in.
It'll scratch more babies.
It'll hunt more strokes
that cat I know.

PC Plod and the Clever Pillar Box

It's snowing out.
Streets are thiefproof.
A wind that blows straight up your nose
and out of your ears.
A night, not fit for a dog to be out, in.

On the corner, PC Plod
brave as a mountain lion and good at sums,
sets the pillar box a simple maths test:
'What is 7 multiplied by 8 minus 56?'

The pillar box was silent for a moment
and then said
Nothing.
'Correct' said Plod
and slouched off towards Bethlehem Avenue.

PC Plod Stumbles Over the Words

Sergeant Large put down his knife and fork
And turning to Plod said 'Yummy yum yum
Yummy yummy yum yum' and began to lick his lips.
'Stop licking my lips' said Plod, and moved further down
   the table.

As he gazed into the middle distance munching a crisp
His reverie was interrupted by a gentle lisp.
It was D.I. Hodges. 'Sorry to disturb you constable,
But I believe I left my taser on the chair behind you.'

As he stood to let her pass, Plod realised
that this was the moment he'd been waiting for.
'I...er...I've got...er...' He stumbled over the words.
The Inspector helped him gently to his feet.

'I've got a spare ticket for the Policeman's Ball
next Saturday, and I was wondering ...'
'I'd love to come with you,' she complied.
'Let's meet outside the Town Hall at 19.00 hrs.'

As Plod watched her exit smartly, the Sergeant
leaned over and nicked a crisp. Winking, he said
'Lucky so and so' and began to squeeze one of his spots.
'Stop squeezing one of my spots' expostulated Plod.

Footie Poem

I'm an ordinary feller six days of the week
But Saturday turn into a football freak
I'm a schizofanatic, sad but it's true
One half of me's red, and the other half's blue.

I can't make me mind up which team to support
Whether to lean to starboard or port
Match day mornings I wake up perplexed
'Cos it's Goodison one week and Anfield the next.

But the worst time of all is Derby day
One half of me's at home and the other's away
So I get down there early in my usual place
With my rainbow scarf and my two-tone face

An I'm shoutin for Liverpool, the Reds can't lose
'Come on Everton'.............. 'Gerrin dere Blues'
'Use your winger'.................'Worra puddin'
'King of the Kop'................. All of a sudden
Wop!.............. 'Goal!' ..... 'Offside!'

And after the match as I walk back alone
It's argue, argue all the way home
Some nights when angry I've even let fly
And given myself a poke in the eye.

But in front of the fire watching Match of the Day
Tired but happy, I look at it this way
Part of me's lost and part of me's won
I've had twice the heartaches, but I've had twice the fun.

Going Through the Old Photos

Who's that?
That's your Auntie Mabel
and that's me
under the table.

Who's that?
That's Uncle Billy.
Who's that?
Me being silly.

Who's that,
licking a lolly?
I'm not sure
but I think it's Polly.

Who's that
behind the tree?
I don't know,
I can't see.
Could be you.
Could be me.

Who's that?
Baby Joe.
Who's that?
I don't know.

Who's that standing
on his head?
Turn it round.
It's Uncle Ted.

The Fight of the Year

And there goes the bell for the third month
and Winter comes out of its corner looking groggy
Spring leads with a left to the head
followed by a sharp right to the body
    daffodils
    primroses
    crocuses
    snowdrops
    lilacs
    violets
    pussywillow
Winter can't take much more punishment
and Spring shows no signs of tiring
    tadpoles
    squirrels
    baalambs
    badgers
    bunny rabbits
    mad march hares
    horses and hounds

Spring is merciless
Winter won't go the full twelve rounds
    bobtail clouds
    scallywaggy winds
    the sun
    a pavement artist
    in every town
A left to the chin
and Winter's down!
    tomatoes
    radish
    cucumber
    onions
    beetroot
    celery
    and any
    amount
    of lettuce
    for dinner
Winter's out for the count
Spring is the winner!

Who's Been at the Toothpaste?

Who's been at the toothpaste?
I know some of you do it right
and you squeeze the tube from the bottom
and you roll up the tube as it gets used up, don't you?

But somebody
somebody here –
you know who you are
you dig your thumb in
anywhere, anyhow
and you've turned that tube of toothpaste
into a squashed sock.
You've made it so hard to use
it's like trying to get toothpaste
out of a packet of nuts.

You know who you are.
I won't ask you to come out here now
but you know who you are.

And then you went and left the top off didn't you?
So the toothpaste turned to cement.

People who do things like that should...
you should be ashamed of yourself.

I am.

A True Story

First love
when I was ten.

We planned a trip
Up to town
Quite a grand thing to do
Up to town
The long ride on the train
all the way
Up to town.

The day before our trip
Up to town
She said, 'Do you mind if Helen
comes with us
Up to town?'
'Great,' I said,
'all three of us, we'll all go
on the train
Up to town.'

So that's how it was —
all three of us,
her, Helen and me,
going on our trip
Up to town.

But when we got
Up to town,
all three of us –
her, Helen and me,

there was this long tunnel
and her friend, Helen,
goes and says:
'Hey – let's run away from him.'
And that's what they did.

So then there wasn't
all three of us any more.
There was just me,
standing in the tunnel.
I didn't chase after them.
I went home.

First Day at School

A millionbillionwillion miles from home
Waiting for the bell to go. (To go where?)
Why are they all so big, other children?
So noisy? So much at home they
Must have been born in uniform
Lived all their lives in playgrounds
Spent the years inventing games
That don't let me in. Games
That are rough, that swallow you up.

And the railings.
All around, the railings.
Are they to keep out wolves and monsters?
Things that carry off and eat children?
Things you don't take sweets from?
Perhaps they're to stop us getting out
Running away from the lessins. Lessin.
What does a lessin look like?
Sounds small and slimy.
They keep them in glassrooms.
Whole rooms made out of glass. Imagine.

I wish I could remember my name
Mummy said it would come in useful.
Like wellies. When there's puddles.
Yellowwellies. I wish she was here.
I think my name is sewn on somewhere
Perhaps the teacher will read it for me.
Tea-cher. The one who makes the tea.

I Used to Have a Little Red Alarm Clock

I used to have a little red alarm clock.
It was my dad's.
He gave me it
and I used to keep it by the side of my bed.

It was very small and it had legs
only the legs were like little marbles –
like little marbles,
and you could unscrew them
out of the bottom of that little red clock.

One morning
I was lying in bed
and I was fiddling with this clock
and I unscrewed one of those
little marble-leg things
and, do you know what I did?
I slipped it into my mouth – to suck,
like a gob-stopper.

Well it was sitting there,
underneath my tongue
when I rolled it over
and – ghulkh – I swallowed it:
the leg off my clock.
It had gone. It was inside me. A piece of metal.

I looked at the clock.
It was leaning over on its side.
I stood it up and of course it fell over.

So I got up,
went downstairs with it
and I was holding it out in front of me
and I walked into the kitchen
and I said:
'Look, the clock. The leg. The leg. The clock – er…'

And my dad took it off me and he said,
'What's up, lad? Did you lose it?
Not to worry, it can't have gone far.
We'll find it,
and we can screw it back on here, look.'

'I swallowed it,' I said.

'You swallowed it? You swallowed it?
Are you mad? Are you stark staring mad?
You've ruined a perfectly good clock.
That was a good clock, that was. Idiot.
Now what's the use of a clock that won't stand up?'
He held it out in front of him,
and he stared at it. I looked at it too.
I was wondering what was happening to the leg.

Wrong

We went on holiday with
Mr Wrong.
Everything we said, he said was
Wrong.

He asked us
if night came before day
or day before night.
We said that day came before night.
He said,
Wrong.

So we said night came before day.
He said,
Wrong.

He asked us which came first,
Sunday or Monday.
We said, Sunday.
He said,
Wrong.

So we said,
Monday.
He said,
Wrong.

He asked us if he was telling fibs.
We said, yes.
He said,
Wrong.

He asked us if he was telling the truth.
We said, yes.
He said,
Wrong.

Then we asked him,
Why are you asking us all these questions?
He said it was because
we liked it.
And we said,
Wrong.

Big Arth

Big Arth from Penarth
was a forward and a half.
Though built like a peninsula
with muscles like pink slagheaps
and a face like a cheese grater
he was as graceful and fast
as a greased cheetah.

A giraffe in the lineout
a rhino in the pack
he never passed forward
when he should have passed back
and once in possession
slalomed his way
through the opposition.

And delicate?
Once for a lark at Cardiff Arms Park
Big Arth converted a soft boiled egg
from the halfway line.
No doubt about it,
he was one of the best players in the second team.

Uncle Sean

If brick-throwing was an Olympic sport
Uncle Sean would be sure to win gold

But it isn't. So he works on a building site
and dreams of glories that might have been

Uncle Sean lives in Coventry
a stone's throw away from the Albert Hall

Where Broccoli Comes From

Not many people know
that broccoli grows in the armpits
of very big green men
who live in the forest,
and brave broccoli cutters
go deep into the forests
and they creep up on
the very big green men.
They wait for the very
big green men
to fall asleep
and the broccoli cutters get out
their great big broccoli razors
and they shave the armpits
of the very big green men.
And that's where broccoli comes from.
Not many people know that.

Just thought I'd let you know.

You Tell Me

When it takes a well-earned rest
Is it still a busy bee?

When a woodcutter chops it down
Is it still a tree?

Do ships wrecked on rugged rocks
Ever forgive the sea?

If it makes them smooth and soft
Would you rub your hands with Glee?

Questions, questions, questions
I've no idea, you tell me.

If you met a tiger in the woods
Would you invite it home for tea?

Would you cuddle a triceratops
Or scream out loud and flee?

Do locks at the end of a boring day
Look forward to the key?

If you found a rattlesnake in baby's cot
Would you shake it or set it free?

Questions, questions, questions
I give in. You tell me.

ROGER McGOUGH is one of Britain's best-loved poets, who also writes for the stage and television. He has been awarded an OBE and a CBE for services to poetry, and was recently honoured with The Freedom of the City of Liverpool. His bestselling books for Frances Lincoln include *An Imaginary Menagerie*, *Lucky*, *Until I Met Dudley* and *Dotty Inventions*. Roger reads and performs his poetry all over the world. He lives in south-west London.

MICHAEL ROSEN is one of the best known
figures in the children's book world and the British
arts scene. He has written numerous award-winning
poetry books, non-fiction and picture books.
He is also a journalist, broadcaster and performer,
who visits schools in the UK and abroad with his one-
man show. He was Children's Laureate from 2007-9,
using the post to be an "ambassador of fun".
He supports Arsenal Football Club and lives
in north London.

KORKY PAUL was born in Zimbabwe. He studied Fine Art at Durban Art School, South Africa and Film Animation at CalArts, California. He began his career in advertising before becoming an illustrator of children's books. He is best known for illustrating the multi-million selling series, *Winnie the Witch*.
He has illustrated two picture books published by Frances Lincoln, *Snail's Legs* by Damian Harvey and *The Very Noisy House* by Julie Rhodes. Known only to himself as the 'World's Greatest Portrait Artist – and Dinosaur Drawer', Korky regularly visits schools promoting his passion for drawing. He is one of the 20% hardcore elite still scribbling with Pen 'n' Ink on Paper. He is a patron of The Art Room and lives in Oxford.

978-1-84780-321-4

Solve riddles, find out how to please a weasel, and discover
what happened to the boy called Lucky.... This brilliant
collection is full of wit, wordplay and wisdom from Roger
McGough, 'the trickster you can trust'.

'A stocking filler that will bring joy all year round is
Roger McGough's superlatively witty, word-loving
collection of poems.' – *The Sunday Times*

978-1-84780-166-1

A witty and wicked collection of poems by Britain's best-loved poet, featuring an amazing A–Z of animals real and imaginary.

'In Roger's menagerie here, you can expect animals that are hybrids of mind-tickling wordplay. In Roger's prankish hands, caterpillar becomes "catopillow" and beware the allivator, that reptile that swallows shoppers at the top of the stairs.' – *The Guardian*